*The
Connell Short Guide
to*

The Suffragettes

by Zoë Thomas

Contents

Introduction	3
When did the suffrage campaigns begin?	5
What was the situation at the turn of the century?	8
The National Union of Women's Suffrage Societies	11
The Women's Social and Political Union	14
Building tensions, 1909-1914	25
Did World War One change suffrage activity?	31
What happened after World War One?	33
Conclusion	35

NOTES

Millicent Garrett Fawcett	*12*
The Pankhursts	*18*
Five facts about Suffrage	*22*
A short chronology	*38*
Further reading	*40*

Introduction

The campaign for female political suffrage which erupted in the years leading up to World War One was the most significant expression of feminist activism in British history. Public fascination with the activities of the suffrage campaigners was fuelled by an outpouring of suffrage autobiographies in the 1920s and 1930s, and, since then, has been kept alive by plentiful books, exhibitions, and most recently the first film, *Suffragette*, released in 2015. Primary sources relating to suffrage are treasured in both national and private archives: they range from photographs and hand-stitched banners through to suffrage-branded dolls, teapots, and board games.

Portrayals of the suffrage movement have been numerous and varied. Many supporters published memoirs to justify their activities. These tended to be romanticised accounts that celebrated individual heroines, rather than comprehensive histories, and they often contradicted one another. Three of the most famous suffragettes, Emmeline Pankhurst and her daughters Christabel and Sylvia, were all leading figures in the militant campaigns and all wrote memoirs that deviated substantially from one another.

Sylvia Pankhurst's 1931 account portrayed her mother negatively, arguing that the activities of working class socialist women – and Sylvia's own role – were what led to the breakthrough in 1918, when the franchise was expanded to include some (though by no means all) women. Emmeline and Christabel Pankhurst, on the other hand, argued that it was the commitment of the militant suffragettes that led to women getting the vote.

As this illustrates, the central disagreement revealed by these memoirs, and by numerous other historical documents, is whether militancy or peaceful activism was the better tactic to use. Suffrage campaigners also disagreed over whether their goal should be securing *all* women the vote, or only those of the middle and upper classes. They disagreed, too, over how much emphasis should be put on changing society in ways which would benefit women as opposed to concentrating entirely on winning them the vote.

The conflicting views of those who were actually involved with the female suffrage campaigns have been echoed down the years in the variety of interpretations put forward by historians. To give a flavour of them this guide looks at three key areas of debate. First, the breadth of the suffrage movement's ambitions. Elizabeth Crawford and Martin Pugh, for example, see the women's suffrage movement as essentially a single-issue political campaign devoted to securing women the vote. Others, such as June Purvis, argue that suffrage campaigners aimed to bring about equality and social change for women on a far broader basis.

The second big issue historians have debated is whether it was the work of the suffrage campaigners or the participation of women during World War One which ultimately led to women getting the vote. The third debate is over the relative effectiveness of the activities of the different groups of suffrage campaigners. Representing these, the two most famous societies were the law-abiding, non-violent National Union of Women's Suffrage Societies (NUWSS), and the militant Women's Social and Political Union (WSPU). The groups disagreed on both the basis of their claims for political power and on the tactics they used to bring about change and historians continue to argue over which one did the most to extend the franchise to women.

When did the suffrage campaigns begin?

The campaign for women's political rights goes back further than most people realise, to the late 18th century. In the early days its advocates were few, but from small beginnings a sense of injustice intensified across the century, and by the 1860s campaigning organisations were blooming among both the middle and the working classes. These were based all over the country, using major cities such as Manchester for public meetings and in which to organise petitions. They had different names and different configurations, but they were united in their main aim: to win women the right to vote through peaceful, constitutional methods.

In 1866 The Women's Suffrage Committee, founded by artist and activist Barbara Bodichon (1827-1891), collected 1,500 signatories for a petition requesting precisely this. John Stuart Mill (1806-1873), the highly respected political economist, philosopher and Liberal Party MP, presented the petition to the House of Commons in 1867. At the same time, he proposed an amendment to the Second Reform Act (1867), arguing that instead of just male householders getting the vote, *all* householders in Britain should be enfranchised, regardless of their sex.

The bill was unsuccessful, but from 1870 to 1884 bills in favour of women's suffrage were presented to Parliament on an almost annual basis. Women campaigners worked hard to keep the issue in the public eye by holding regular public meetings and publishing pamphlets, leaflets and journals. They concentrated particularly on Parliamentary proceedings because these were extensively covered in the regional and national press.

In 1869, John Stuart Mill laid out his argument for "perfect equality" between the sexes in his essay *The Subjection of Women*. He wrote that the subordination of women was "one of the chief hindrances to human improvement" and should be ended on the grounds of social justice. His liberal feminist position represented the views of many suffragist campaigners and his essay remained very popular for the next 50 years.

There were, however, suffrage groups with different preoccupations. Socialist feminists, in particular, devoted much of their energy to attacking the economic inequality resulting from the British class system. They considered it crucial to take into account class as well as gender in debates about female political emancipation. As historian Sue Bruley notes: "Socialist-feminists... believed that ultimately women could only be emancipated in a socialist society." In contrast to this, liberal feminists were often perceived to be concerned only with the rights and needs of middle-class women.

Just as they do today, feminists in the 19th and early 20th centuries had very different ideas about equality and women's rights. Women's consciousness of their gender co-existed in different ways with their sense of class identity and political party loyalty and they had a wide range of ideas about the appropriate social roles for men and women. The Women's Franchise League, a female suffrage society set up in 1889, was seen as radical because it included married women in its demand for the vote. Other more cautious suffragettes supported married women's exclusion. Similarly, many campaigners did not want gender differences to be extinguished. Instead they argued that female enfranchisement was needed so that women could perform their gendered role more effectively, using their nurturing and womanly nature to help bring about social reforms. Others still assumed a basic human equality between men and women. "Feminist ideology took different forms," Sue Bruley writes, "and there was not one but many feminisms."

What was the situation at the turn of the century?

Victorian women had very few civil or political rights. Until the Married Women's Property Act was passed in 1882, married women belonged to their husbands in the eyes of the law. The 1882 act significantly improved their position as it allowed married women to own and control their own property.

By the turn of the century further gains had been made. Government involvement in state life had grown considerably, which meant more officials were needed to run local services. Slowly, women began to gain power within the expanded local organisations, among them the church and those devoted to education and social reform. In 1894 the requirement that **Poor Law Guardians** must own property was removed, enabling married women to stand for this important office.[*] Women

---

[*] **Poor Law Guardians** were people elected to sit on the Boards of Guardians that administered the parish workhouses. By 1895 there were 802 female guardians in Britain

who did so included some from the working classes, such as Selina Cooper from Burnley. From 1907 women ratepayers could also stand in borough and county council elections, although few were successful and only around 50 women had become borough or county councillors by 1914.

By the early 20th century, then, it was deemed more or less acceptable for women to have a position in local government services. National politics, on the other hand, was seen differently. Many still believed that national politics was a man's world, and continued to promote the well-established ideology of "public/private" spheres, arguing that women should be based in the home whilst men should hold public roles in society. Various anti-suffrage arguments were put forward, drawing attention to women's apparent inferiority to men: their lack of education, fears about women neglecting their home or children, limited experiences of work and a supposed inability to defend their country.

The Conservative statesman Lord Curzon declared in 1912 that women "do not have the experience to be able to vote". He dwelt on women's physical weaknesses and warned people that women might not vote for the Conservatives (which, he felt, would have a detrimental effect on government and on society). Taking what was a common line of argument, he used war as a way to highlight how women could not be ranked with men: "What is the good of talking about the equality of the sexes? The first whiz of the bullet, the first boom of the cannon and where is the equality of the sexes then?"

Despite such strong opposition, suffrage campaigners kept up the pressure. At the turn of the century, writes the historian Harold Smith, "diverse groups of women had concluded that the world would be a better place if they possessed the franchise", regardless of whether they believed they had the "same inherent rights as men or whether they thought that women had unique concerns as wives and mothers". To understand how truly radical this sense of female entitlement to suffrage was, it is important to remember that many working-class men still did not have the vote before 1918 either, because men had to own property to be able to vote.

The franchise was, however, slowly extended in the 19th century to include more men, via the Second Reform Act (1867) and the Third Reform Act (1884). By 1900, on average, two out of three working men could vote. The fact that this figure now included some working-class men heightened a sense of the hypocrisy of the situation. Middle-class women were denied the right to vote but in many ways their circumstances were similar: they were ratepayers and subject to the same laws of the land.

The National Union of Women's Suffrage Societies

In 1897 all of the regional suffrage societies were brought together under the umbrella organisation of the National Union of Women Suffrage Societies (NUWSS), which aimed to have a branch in every constituency in Britain. Officially, the NUWSS pursued a non-party policy, offering help in the elections to any candidate who planned to support women's suffrage. In fact, a number of prominent Liberals dominated its leadership. After the death of one of them – Lydia Becker – in 1890, the president of the society for the next 20 years was tireless campaigner Millicent Garrett Fawcett (1847-1929), who had published and lectured extensively on female suffrage.

Members of the NUWSS thought that the best way to achieve political change for women was to target parliament through peaceful persuasion and at the same time to educate the public. They were active in lobbying individual MPs known to be sympathetic to their cause, encouraging them to raise the issue of women's suffrage in debates on the floor of the House. Their aim was to build, through this, an all-party body of support for a **private member women's suffrage bill.***

---

* A **private member's bill** is a proposed law put forward in Parliament by an MP who is not a member of the Cabinet.

The NUWSS concentrated its efforts on demanding equal voting rights for women under the existing franchise laws, which at this point required electors to be property holders. This tactic went against the views of those in the Labour and Socialist movements, who aimed to achieve suffrage for all adults, regardless of financial income or property ownership. Many NUWSS members did hope for a full democratic franchise eventually, but thought it necessary to establish sexual equality first, before campaigning for voting rights for working-class women.

MILLICENT GARRETT FAWCETT

Millicent Garrett Fawcett was brought up in Suffolk in a family where she and her siblings were encouraged to have an active interest in political issues. Her older sister Elizabeth Garrett Anderson (1836-1917) went to London and became the first female doctor in Britain. Millicent joined her, aged 12, when she was sent to study at a private boarding school in Blackheath. This education gave her a life-long interest in education and literature. During her teenage years, another sister, Louise, took Millicent to see John Stuart Mill speak in support of women's rights, which profoundly influenced her. She was also introduced to Henry Fawcett (1833-1884), MP for Brighton and a supporter of women's votes. He had been blinded in a shooting accident in 1857 and had been supposed to marry Millicent's older sister Elizabeth. Elizabeth, however, decided that she wanted to devote herself to medicine, Millicent and Henry became close and, although he was 14 years her senior, they married in 1867.

A prolific writer of articles

The NUWSS used leaflets, petitions, letters and rallies as its key tactics to gain votes for women. From 1897 to 1903 it consisted of a federation of 16 societies, but, by 1909, another 45 had been set up under its auspices. In the same year the NUWSS established its own journal, *The Common Cause*, edited by Cambridge-educated pacifist and feminist Helena Swanwick (1864-1939).

The organisation continued to grow fast. By 1911 there were 305 societies, and by 1913, 400. Joyce Marlow presents the popular view that it was the law-abiding strategies of the NUWSS, not the

---

and books (including *Lectures on Political Subjects* and *Political Economy for Beginners*), Millicent was also involved in the establishment of women's colleges such as Newnham College at the University of Cambridge. She could often be found sitting in the Ladies' Gallery at the House of Commons eagerly watching political debates.

Although a strong advocate for the NUWSS, she campaigned for a wide variety of causes – not just the vote for women. She helped to support Josephine Butler in her campaign to stop white slave trade trafficking, for example, and Clementina Black's efforts to help low-paid women workers. Although she was a Liberal she became increasingly frustrated with the Liberal Party's lack of support for female franchise. She remained committed to constitutional methods to gain votes, but she admired the courage of the suffragettes.

When all women over 21 finally got the franchise in 1928 Millicent was allowed to attend Parliament to see the vote take place. She wrote that night in her diary: "It is almost exactly 61 years ago since I heard John Stuart Mill introduce his suffrage amendment to the Reform Bill on May 20th, 1867. So I have had extraordinary good luck in having seen the struggle from the beginning." ■

headline-grabbing militancy of the suffragettes that ultimately won the day:

> ...for every suffragette there were always dozens of non-militant suffragists. Some would argue – including me – that it was the moderates of the NUWSS, led by Millicent Fawcett, who actually won the vote.

As we will be see, not all historians agree with this interpretation.

The Women's Social and Political Union

The Women's Social and Political Union (WSPU) was a women's suffrage society founded in Manchester on 10th October 1903 at the home of Emmeline Pankhurst. Unlike the NUWSS, which allowed male members, the WSPU was female only. Supporters of the organisation were frustrated that even though private member's bills on female suffrage had been presented to Parliament every year since 1900 nothing had happened. One bill on women's suffrage in 1904 was so unpopular that MPs resorted to discussing the contents of the previous bill – concerning tail lights on cars – for hours in order to avoid it. Early supporters of the WSPU were often working-class socialist women, such as the seamstress Hannah Mitchell (1872-1956) and the mill worker Annie Kenney (1879-1953).

The WSPU was initially formed to run in close connection to the infant **Independent Labour Party**, of which Emmeline Pankhurst was an active member.* The link distinguished it sharply from the non-partisan NUWSS and created a struggle within Labour Party councils about whether or not Labour should support women's suffrage. Some Labour members and their socialist supporters felt that the battle at this point should be fought solely for full male suffrage: the first aim, they argued, must be to ensure that the vote was not restricted to wealthy men who owned property.

Women's suffrage supporters, however, such as the Labour MP Keir Hardie (1856-1915), often spoke in the Commons on the subject and attended WSPU events. The Labour MP George Lansbury (1859-1940) went even further, resigning his seat so that he could fight a by-election on the suffrage question. He was imprisoned in 1913 after making a speech at a WSPU rally in support of the suffragettes' campaign of arson attacks.

The Pankhursts quickly decided that up till now women's suffrage campaigners had not been

---

* Established in 1893, the **Independent Labour Party** was affiliated to the Labour Party from 1906 to 1932. After that it stood on its own until 1975, then was renamed Independent Labour Publications and absorbed into the Labour Party as a pressure group.

extreme enough in their tactics, and the WSPU became the leading militant group in Britain. Susan Kingsley Kent writes that "with the arrival of the WSPU... the suffrage campaign took on new life and meaning", and, although historians debate how effective its tactics actually were, it is certainly true that the style of campaigning changed. The Pankhursts' intentions were encapsulated in their slogan "Deeds not words", which they plastered on banners, mastheads, and later on the paper wrapped around the stones they threw. They developed a striking colour scheme of purple, white, and green: purple for dignity, white for purity, and green for fertility and hope for the future.

Militancy began in October 1905 in the Free Trade Hall in Manchester. WSPU members Christabel Pankhurst and Annie Kenney demanded at a rally that the Liberal MP Sir Edward Grey (1862-1933) and Liberal candidate Winston Churchill (1874-1965) reveal their stance on women's suffrage and refused to leave when they got no response. They unfurled a "Votes for Women" flag and were physically thrown out of the hall by stewards. They then staged an impromptu meeting on the steps, at which point Christabel Pankhurst spat on a policeman. After failing to pay the subsequent fines, the two women ended up in jail. This unprecedented act, and the women's treatment at the hands of men, were widely reported in the press, encouraging many more women to become involved in the cause.

Annie Kenney and Christabel Pankhurst, c.1908 (wikicommons)

From this point onwards the WSPU was acutely attuned to the power of militancy to attract newspaper coverage. This militancy has also attracted a lot of scholarly notice. June Purvis suggests that it is the illegal "militant" activities that have captured the imagination of historians in the past and present rather than the rather more law-abiding tactics implemented by the constitutional National Union of Women's Suffrage Societies.

Sandra Stanley Bolton is one of several historians who argue that the spectacle of respectable, middle-class women engaging in physical violence and organising mass political events created a huge sense of shock across British society, and this shock value was the most powerful campaigning tactic for the WSPU. Others, however, such as Joyce Marlow, assess the more gradual, less spectacular methods of the suffragists as more effective in the long run.

In 1906 Emmeline and Christabel Pankhurst decided to move the WSPU's headquarters to London, the nation's political centre. They acquired a property near the law courts in Holborn. Sylvia Pankhurst was already based in London studying art and campaigning with Teresa Billington-Greig (1877-1964), another suffrage organiser. Sylvia

THE PANKHURSTS

The Pankhurst family has dominated commentary on female suffrage in Britain. In 1999, for example, *Time* magazine named Emmeline one of their "100 Most Important People of the 20th Century", saying that "she shaped an idea of women for our time; she shook society into a new pattern from which there could be no going back".

Emmeline Pankhurst (1858-1928) came from a strongly political background. Her father Robert Goulden campaigned against slavery and her mother Sophia Crane was a feminist who took Emmeline to women's suffrage meetings from an early age. Sophia had been born on the Isle of Man and kept a family holiday home there – this was important because the Isle of Man had granted suffrage to women property owners in 1881 and so Emmeline grew up with a strong awareness of the inequality of women elsewhere in Britain.

At 20, Emmeline married the barrister and legal reformer Richard Pankhurst (1835-1898), 24 years her senior. Richard was heavily involved in

Pankhurst and Billington-Greig had up to this point mainly been trying to help working-class women in the East End of London.

Following their move to London, the Pankhursts met wealthy suffragette Emmeline Pethick-Lawrence (1867–1954) who was involved in benevolent work for working-class women, alongside her husband Frederick Pethick-Lawrence (1871–1961), a radical lawyer. Emmeline Pethick-Lawrence became the treasurer for the WSPU, and helped to recruit a number of well-off socialites to

supporting women's rights. He had drafted the first Women's Suffrage Bill in 1869 and had been responsible for the Married Women's Property Act of 1884. Together, the Pankhursts created the Women's Suffrage League in 1889 and were active members of the Independent Labour Party. Their family home at Nelson Street in Manchester is now a museum, the Pankhurst Centre.

In 1903, after the death of Richard, Emmeline set up the WSPU. Her daughters Christabel (1880-1958), Sylvia (1882-1960), and Adela (1885-1961) were all closely involved from the beginning, although Sylvia left in 1914 out of frustration at how the WSPU was being run, and Adela, equally at odds with the WSPU by this time, emigrated to Australia, also in 1914. The daughters had wished to pursue other careers – Christabel as a dancer and Sylvia as an artist – but they got swept into the suffrage campaigns and dedicated their lives to improving women's rights. The family, however, often disagreed on tactics and sometimes fell out with one another. Christabel was strongly pro-war and principally interested in winning the vote for middle-class women, while Sylvia was a pacifist who was dedicated to helping working-class women. ■

the organisation. She also co-ran the WSPU's new journal, *Votes for Women,* with her husband.

Opposition to women's suffrage, meanwhile, was gaining strength in the Labour and Socialist movements. The issue of female votes was seen as a distraction from the most important goal: securing equal political rights for all men. In response to this hostility, in October 1906 Christabel Pankhurst announced that the WSPU would no longer be supporting Labour Party candidates. A number of socialist suffragists amongst the leaders of the WSPU, including the philanthropist Charlotte Despard (1884-1939) and campaigner Anne Cobden Sanderson (1853-1926), were extremely concerned by this change of tack and tried to reverse it. At the Independent Labour Party conference in 1907, however, Emmeline Pankhurst reaffirmed the WSPU's policy change. Charlotte Despard and Annie Cobden Sanderson were equally adamant in their determination to continue to support Labour candidates. Tensions grew and the dissidents finally decided to establish a new organisation, separate to the WSPU, which they entitled the Women's Freedom League.

Unlike the NUWSS, but like the WSPU, the Women's Freedom League broke laws, but it tended to use direct action (resisting paying tax, for example, and refusing to co-operate with census-taking), rather than attacking property and people. It also had a more democratic structure than the

WSPU, whose dictatorial leadership had long frustrated many potential and actual supporters.

Some years later, in January 1914, Sylvia Pankhurst and the East End branch of the WSPU also decided to break away from the main WSPU organisation, feeling that it was becoming too wrapped up in the needs of middle-class women. Sylvia formed the East London Federation of Suffragettes to concentrate more fully on the rights of working-class women, as well as on improving their pay and working conditions, securing them proper housing and protecting their children's health.

Despite these defections, the WSPU organised a number of high-profile parades and demonstrations, attracting huge crowds. On 21st June 1908 a suffrage demonstration bigger than any previous such gathering took place in Hyde Park, a day which was later dubbed "Women's Sunday". Trains were specially chartered to help suffrage supporters attend from all over Britain. There were singers, banner parades, brass bands, and 20 platforms erected in a circle across the park to enable 80 speakers to address the masses.

Suffragettes also headed vast processions on horseback: one member, Elsie Howey (1884-1963), led a demonstration in 1909 dressed as Joan of Arc. These women used what historian Lisa Tickner has famously termed "suffrage spectacle" to encourage public interest in the campaigns.

FIVE FACTS ABOUT SUFFRAGE

1.

Members of The Women's Social and Political Union (WSPU) used all sorts of tactics to infiltrate Parliament, disguising themselves and even donning the outfits of messenger boys and waitresses. Suffragist Ray Strachey (1887-1940) said they "sprang out of organ lofts, they peered through roof windows, and leapt out of innocent looking furniture vans; they materialised on station platforms, they harangued the terrace of the House from the river, and wherever they were least expected there they were".

2.

Before 1834 women were made to watch proceedings in the House of Commons via a ventilation shaft in the ceiling. A Ladies' Gallery was created for the new Palace of Westminster, built after the fire of 1834, but the windows were covered with heavy metal grilles which made it hard for women to listen to, or even see, the debates taking place. Suffragist Millicent Garrett Fawcett said that the grille was "like using a gigantic pair of spectacles which did not fit, and made the Ladies' Gallery a grand place for getting headaches".

3.
Daily Mail journalist Charles E. Hands coined "suffragettes" as a term of derision, but the WSPU quickly claimed it as a way to differentiate their activities from the non-militant suffragists.

4.
Despite her role as a female figurehead, Queen Victoria showed her disapproval of suffrage campaigners, bemoaning the "mad, wicked folly of Women's Rights with all its attendant horrors, on which my poor feeble sex is bent, forgetting every sense of womanly feelings and propriety".

5.
After the vote was won, militant suffragettes Christabel and Emmeline Pankhurst decided to open a tea shop together on the French Rivera in 1925. This venture was unsuccessful and they both returned to England the following year.

Poster for the Artists' Suffrage League, c.1910–1919

Building tensions, 1909-1914

The differences between suffragists and suffragettes have often been portrayed as clear-cut. Until the summer of 1909, however, the suffragettes were less radical than they later became. They concentrated their efforts on obstructing political meetings, heckling cabinet ministers, and marching to parliament to try and meet MPs. Historians such as Ann Morley and Liz Stanley find that up to this point the dividing line between the "militants" and the "constitutionalists" (the NUWSS) was actually quite blurred. The societies continued to overlap until 1912 at least, with non-militants often providing assistance for the militants' activities until the latter started to commit arson.

But, as Krista Cowman writes, "there were very real differences in policy and tactics between the suffrage organisations of Edwardian Britain". These became increasingly apparent after 1909. Militants began to throw stones to break the windows of government offices in a new and (as they saw it) "symbolic" protest against the politicians who still refused to meet them to discuss their demands. The appointment of the Liberal Herbert Henry Asquith (1852-1928) as Prime Minister further antagonised the suffragettes, especially as Asquith – who, unlike many in his party, was decidedly anti-women's suffrage – said that he was going to put forward a measure to extend the vote to all men. In 1909 Marion Wallace Dunlop (1864-1942), sculptor and illustrator, was the first woman to go on hunger strike. After 91 hours of fasting in Holloway prison she was released. From this point on, numerous suffragettes used hunger striking as a political statement to show their anger at the government.

Tensions grew further after the 1910 Conciliation Bill was read in Parliament. The bill was put forward to extend voting rights to one million wealthy, property-owning women, but, although given a second reading, it failed to become law. The prime minister said it was taking too much parliamentary time and in the end it was abandoned.

The bill shows what a complex issue women's suffrage had become. Some MPs opposed it simply because they did not want any women to get the vote; other *pro*-suffrage MPs opposed it because they thought the stipulations were too narrow as it was only aimed at enfranchising wealthy women. Numerous Liberal MPs also opposed it because they thought these well-off women would go on to vote for the Conservative Party. Meanwhile, the government was distracted, and facing all sorts of other crises, above all bubbling political tension in Ireland.

Bitterly disappointed by the failure of the Conciliation Bill, the WSPU sent 300 women to protest, which led to violent clashes outside Parliament on 18th November 1910. The date has since been labelled "Black Friday". The suffragettes marched to Parliament Square where they were stopped by plain-clothed and uniformed police officers who had been ordered not to let them approach the Houses of Parliament. For the next six hours the women suffered from violent treatment at the hands of police officers and male bystanders. There were said to be numerous deliberate acts of cruelty, and one woman, Cecilia Haig (1862-1912), died from the injuries she sustained. Susan Kingsley Kent has suggested, however, that, although horrific, these displays of violence against women "served as powerful recruiting agents for the suffrage cause" as "militants and non-militants alike expressed appreciation that the 'brute' sexuality of men had finally been exposed".

From 1912 onwards, the WSPU took its militant tactics even further. Emmeline Pankhurst argued that this was a reasonable response to the frustration felt by people who had now been campaigning for 50 years for votes for women. She justified her actions by declaring:

> We have tried every way, but we have had contempt poured upon us. Violence is the only way that we have to get the power that every citizen should have.

WSPU members began to attack property, carrying out secret arson attacks, vandalising post boxes and smashing windows. The first widespread window-smashing took place in London's West End in 1912. Windows were broken at numerous stores, including Harrods.

During these years, one suffragette, Kitty Marion (1871-1944), burned down a racecourse grandstand while another, Mary Richardson (1882–1961), slashed the *Rokeby Venus* in the National Gallery to protest about Emmeline Pankhurst being force-fed. She said to the WSPU afterwards:

> I have tried to destroy the picture of the most beautiful woman in mythological history as a protest against the Government for destroying Mrs. Pankhurst, who is the most beautiful character in modern history.

In June 1913 the suffragette Emily Wilding Davison (1872-1913) was killed when she stepped in front of King George V's horse at the Epsom Derby. Although initially she was thought to have committed suicide, it is now widely believed that she was trying to disrupt the race and to tie a scarf in suffragette colours to the horse. She is commonly remembered as the "suffragette martyr". In the same year Emmeline Pankhurst helped organise a group that set fire to the house that was being built for the Chancellor of the Exchequer, David Lloyd George.

The government began to implement more and more measures to stop the WSPU. Emmeline

Pankhurst and the Pethick-Lawrences were put on trial for conspiracy, and *Votes for Women*, the suffrage journal, was censored. In 1913 the so-called "Cat and Mouse Act" was introduced. Officially known as the Prisoners (Temporary Discharge for Ill-Health) Act, this decreed that suffragettes who were on hunger strike in prison could be released as soon as they appeared to be weak or ill. Yet once they had recovered the act allowed police officers to imprison them again. It seemed to the general public to resemble the actions of a cat playing with a mouse.

Suffrage supporter and composer Ethel Smyth (1858-1944) described the act as "hideous":

> The authorities dared not let the women die, so would release them, sometimes half-dead, to be rearrested as soon as they were judged fit to serve the remainder of their sentence.

Some of the imprisoned women were force fed, instead of being released, a policy the Home Secretary at the time, Reginald McKenna (1863-1943), tried to justify by saying that the only alternative to forced feeding was to "let the prisoners die". As portrayed in the recent film *Suffragette*, the forced feeding of these women was a brutal and life-threatening procedure.

Predictably perhaps, class tensions surfaced in the treatment of prisoners. Wealthy WSPU supporter Lady Constance Lytton grew concerned that working-class women were being treated far worse than middle and upper class women in prison. So she disguised herself as a seamstress and had herself arrested and sent to prison, where, as she'd expected, she was treated notably less well than before, and forcibly fed several times before being recognised and released.

In 1913 the NUWSS abandoned its long-term strategy of trying to gain suffrage support through private member bills in parliament. Instead it began to push for a government measure that would include women. The initiative was supported at Labour's annual conference, at which the party declared that it would now support women's suffrage. In the summer of 1913 the NUWSS staged a massive "pilgrimage" of suffragists, leaving from 17 cities across Britain with London the final meeting place. After a surfeit of sensational stories about the WSPU, the NUWSS thought that the public needed reminding about its work as a much larger and non-militant movement. One of the pilgrimage organisers felt that "the enormous educational work that is being done by many thousands of peaceful, law-abiding suffragists" ought to be promoted above the suffragettes' exhibitionism.

In 1914, as the Liberals prepared for a general election, the mood in Parliament was becoming increasingly supportive of women's suffrage. It was felt that there was a need for radical reform of the franchise and that this must now include women. A group of MPs, Lloyd George among them, opened discussions with the NUWSS for the first time, and prepared a new reform bill that would include women's suffrage. Their preparations, however, were interrupted by the outbreak of war in August 1914.

Did World War One change suffrage activity?

At the outbreak of war, then, women were still voteless, parliament having rejected every women's suffrage bill it had considered. And when war began WSPU leaders Emmeline and Christabel Pankhurst called an immediate halt to militancy and instead encouraged women to switch their efforts to war work as a way to win enfranchisement. In 1917 they relaunched the WSPU under the title the Women's Party, and Christabel Pankhurst stood, unsuccessfully, in the 1918 general election.

The majority of the other women's suffrage organisations, including the NUWSS, also chose to devote their energies to supporting the war effort, although NUWSS campaigning for female suffrage did still continue. During 1916 and 1917 the House of Commons Speaker, James Lowther (1855-1949), chaired a conference about electoral reform that recommended limited suffrage for women. Pre-war hostility had lessened, but there was still concern that if universal suffrage were implemented, female voters would outnumber men.

War brought about new problems as well. In the NUWSS there were significant differences between the women who were pacifists and those who supported the war effort. In 1915, NUWSS leader Millicent Garrett Fawcett refused to let the NUWSS take part in an international conference for women in The Hague to try and bring the end to the war, and most of the executive committee subsequently resigned.

Between 1914 and 1918 an estimated two million women replaced men in the British work force. The proportion of women in total employment went from 24 per cent in July 1914 to 37 per cent by November 1918. Although women's roles in war were repeatedly stated to be only "for the duration", there was a new involvement of women in public life, often in jobs that they previously had not been doing (such as in munitions factories and replacing farm workers in the Women's Land Army). Many have argued that this significantly changed perceptions about the role of women in British society. It is important to note, however, that although women had "proved" that they were capable of working in a range of jobs that were considered to be outside the feminine comfort zone, employers still paid them far less than men.

Women at work in a munitions factory, c.1917

What happened after World War One?

In 1917 the government decided on franchise reform to ensure there was suffrage for all soldiers. At this point only 58 per cent of the adult male population had the right to vote. The female suffrage organisations demanded that women should be included in the reform, and for the first time were accorded a positive response. In May 1917 the Representation of the People Bill passed through the Commons with a large majority, and it became law in 1918. Altogether, the Representation of the People Act expanded the electorate from eight to 21 million. The fact that it included women *at all* was a radical new departure – but it did not bring equality.

To vote, women had to be aged 30 or above *and*

local government electors or the wives of such electors: 8.5 million women met this criterion, representing only 40 per cent of the total adult female population of the country. This was a stark contrast to the reform for men, which extended the vote to *all* men over the age of 21, and to military veterans aged 19 or above. Many of the women who had served their country during the war as munitions workers were typically under 30 and unmarried, and were therefore not enfranchised. The new female electorate in 1918 comprised predominantly middle-aged, middle-class, Conservative women.

The act was a compromise, and, as Amanda Vickery has pointed out, "fell short of what had been promised". The NUWSS leadership nonetheless lent its support to the compromise, pleased that some women had now been enfranchised. They decided, however, to rename their organisation the National Union of Societies for Equal Citizenship, and that their aim from now on must be to secure *all* women the vote. Under the new leadership of Eleanor Rathbone (1872-1946), they continued to argue for women's rights, whilst at the same time pursuing equality in the franchise laws. The latter goal was finally achieved in 1928 with the Equal Franchise Act. This gave the vote to all women over the age of 21.

Historians continue to this day to debate why it was that some women got the vote in 1918. Martin Pugh attributes the achievement to the war and the activities of the NUWSS. The Great War did create unprecedented opportunities for women to prove themselves as worthy citizens, and Pugh feels that "by 1900 the NUWSS had won over the anti-suffragists to their cause". Controversially, he finds that "the militancy of the suffragettes was counter-productive in that it alienated MPs".

Harold Smith, conversely, uses the limitations of female suffrage in 1918, with many women involved in the war effort excluded, to suggest that the vote was not a reward for female patriotic contribution. He and other historians have argued that there were in fact a wide variety of reasons for the passing of the act in 1918. Brian Harrison, for example, points out that the war years witnessed the removal of a number of obstacles to reform: the WSPU abandoned its militant tactics; anti-suffrage Prime Minister Herbert Asquith resigned in 1916; and the formation of a coalition government the same year eased political fears about the suffrage issue being used to benefit one party over another.

Conclusion

The campaign for women's suffrage was the biggest mass movement to improve women's rights that has ever been seen in Britain. The task of uncovering the "true" history of the campaign remains a contentious one even now. In particular, the relative importance of the "militants" and the "constitutionalists" still has remarkable potential to divide opinion. Historians, politicians and scholars have all asserted their own views about key figures such as the Pankhursts, Millicent Garrett Fawcett, and the anti-suffrage Prime Minister Herbert Henry Asquith.

As one might expect, the way that the fight for suffrage has been portrayed has varied in line with the culture and mood of the times. After World War One, for example, there was a backlash against the militancy of suffrage campaigners. In a conservative, war-torn society keen to refrain from further violence, many wished to re-establish traditional gendered roles as men came back from fighting. Some, more recently, have even questioned the impact the vote actually had on women, especially working-class women. There is still much research to be done on this and on the suffrage campaigns. As Sandra Stanley Holton argues:

> there are ample seams of evidence yet to be
> mined, many questions yet to be answered, and
> any number of new stories to be told – the
> kaleidoscope keeps on turning.

The way films have depicted women's fight for suffrage provides an interesting insight into feminism and the British cultural consciousness. The 1964 film *Mary Poppins,* for example, included the character of Mrs. Banks, who repeatedly left her children at home to devote her energies to the cause, singing the pro-suffrage pastiche song "We're clearly soldiers in petticoats...dauntless crusaders for women's votes". Yet it was not until almost a hundred years after the campaigns, in 2015, that the first film was made which dealt fully and seriously with the topic. *Suffragette* depicted the realities of suffrage campaigning and the activities of its foot soldiers in the working classes. The film highlighted the daily dilemmas faced by the suffragettes as having been immediate, exhausting and extraordinarily important. Departing from the examination of middle-class women which has often been emphasised in suffrage literature, the film revolved, in particular, around the activities of an East London laundry worker called Maud. It strove to show the complexities behind the campaigns, including both male suffragettes and women-hating men.

The contemporary feminist group Sisters Uncut used the film's premiere to promote its campaign against female domestic abuse: more than a hundred protestors jumped onto the red carpet and set off purple and green smoke bombs outside the Odeon cinema in London. They were, they said, using "suffragette methods to declare that as long as violence against women continues, the battle for women's liberation has not yet been won". These activists provide a sobering reminder of the continued fight by many for women's equality today, and of the continued relevance of studying and debating the history of the suffrage campaigners.

A SHORT CHRONOLOGY

1868 First ever public meeting about women's suffrage in Manchester.

1869 Publication of John Stuart Mill's *The Subjection of Women*.

1870 The first women's suffrage bill rejected by Parliament.

1878 London University allows women to graduate.

1897 The NUWSS formed.

1903 The WSPU formed.

1905 Christabel Pankhurst and Annie Kenney imprisoned for interrupting a meeting of the Liberal Party.

1906 The first march of women to lobby Parliament, organised by the WSPU.

1908 Herbert Henry Asquith becomes Liberal prime minister,

1909 Agitation grows. Window-breaking, and the first hunger strike led by Marion Dunlop are followed by forced feeding of other hunger strikers.

1912 First serious act of arson by Helen Craggs.

1913 Passing of the "Cat and Mouse" Act.

1913 Emily Davison killed at Epsom Derby.

1914 World War One begins and militant activities stop.

1918 Representation of the People Act gives the vote to women over the age of 30 who own houses, are the wives of house owners, own property worth more than £5 or are graduates of a university.

1919 Lady Astor becomes the first woman MP.

1928 Equal Franchise Act grants the vote to all women over the age of 21.

FURTHER READING

Elizabeth Crawford, *The Women's Suffrage Movement: A Reference Guide, 1866-1928* (1999)

Lyndsey Jenkins, *Lady Constance Lytton: Aristocrat, Suffragette, Martyr* (2015)

Annie Kenney, *Memories of a Militant* (1924)

Jill Liddington and Jill Norris, *One Hand Tied Behind Us: The Rise of the Women's Suffrage Movement* (1978)

Hannah Mitchell (Ed. Geoffrey Mitchell), *The Hard Way Up: The Autobiography of Hannah Mitchell, Suffragette and Rebel* (1968)

Sylvia Pankhurst, *The Suffragette Movement* (1932)

Martin Pugh, *The Pankhursts* (2001)

Sandra Stanley Holton, *Suffrage Days: Stories from the Women's Suffrage Movement* (1996)

Ray Strachey, *The Cause: A Short History of the Women's Movement in Great Britain* (1928)

Lisa Tickner, *The Spectacle of Women* (1987)

First published in 2016 by
Connell Guides
Artist House
35 Little Russell Street
London WC1A 2HH

10 9 8 7 6 5 4 3 2 1

Copyright © Connell Guides Publishing Ltd.
All rights reserved. No part of this publication
may be reproduced, stored in a retrieval system or transmitted in any
form, or by any means (electronic, mechanical, or otherwise) without
the prior written permission of both the copyright owners
and the publisher.

All images used in this book are considered to be in the public domain.
Picture sources:
p.17 Wikicommons
p.24 Wikicommons / Library of Congress
p.33 Wikicommons / Imperial War Museum

A CIP catalogue record for this book is available from the British Library.
ISBN 978-1-911187-35-6

Design © Nathan Burton
Assistant Editors:
Paul Woodward & Brian Scrivener

Printed in Great Britain

www.connellguides.com